WAY OF THE RAVEN

TOMAHAWK COMBATIVES

by

FERNAN VARGAS, MASTER AT ARMS

WAR HAWK

WAY OF THE RAVEN
TOMAHAWK COMBATIVES VOLUME ONE

BY
Fernan Vargas

With contributing author James Smith & Snake Blocker

Foreword by Snake Blocker

Cover Model: Grand Master Black Hawk Walters

Photo Models: Manley Blackman, Sahnya Thom, Chris Santos, Mohammed Martinez, Armando Bucio, David Woulard, Eric Kaplan & George Tellez, Anthony Calderone, Phil Elmore, Col. Dwight Mclemore

WAR HAWK

WAY OF THE RAVEN

TOMAHAWK COMBATIVES VOLUME ONE

Copyright© 2017

First Printing 2017

Raven Tactical International

Chicago, Illinois USA

www.RavenTactical.com

"AN AXE WITHOUT A SHAFT
IS NO THREAT TO A FOREST."
-ALBERT EINSTEIN

FOREWORD

BY
SNAKE BLOCKER, LIPAN APACHE TRIBE OF TEXAS

Any serious martial artist, survivalists, fighter, law enforcer, security officer, or self-defense practitioner must add a level of knowledge of the tomahawk along their journey in life. Many versions of the tomahawk have been around since the first people in 'time-immemorial.' The tomahawk (hawk) is merely a tool. Its use is determined by the hand, or hands that wield it. For a survivalist, it can cut timber to feed a fire. It can chop a tree to build shelter. It can cut the limbs of a trophy Elk to transport section by section back to base camp. For a martial artist, it can defeat a larger opponent, or several larger opponents. The tomahawk is neither savvy, nor cunning. It is neither righteous, nor wrong. Its fate is in the use, or misuse of its holder. Its fear-factor is in the eye of its beholder or receiver. I can write a volume of books on the many uses of the mighty tomahawk, but no need to state the obvious applications. If you aim to learn self-defense, you must learn the tomahawk, because violence has been around since Cain killed Able. Learn from the respected instructors, then battle-test what works for you.

What worked for Goyathlay (Geronimo) may not work for you, my warrior friend. What works for you, may not work for Justin Beaver. Everyone must take a drill and make adaptations to meet their own individual skill set and limitations. Everyone has a different range of motion; a different arm length; different wrist strength; a different walking or running gait; different mobility, and a different speed. Add a variety of tomahawk books and videos to your library of weapons and you will be leaps ahead of the average Joe. The hawk, like the knife, has always been around, and it is not going away. Most assaults around the world are not the result of firearms, but rather a result of hand held weapons, which include: knives, sticks, clubs, bats, and tomahawks. No great library is complete without including some material to cover this topic.

I lived in the Middle East for over 3 years and I saw tomahawks in Kuwait, Iraq, and Afghanistan. I lived in Los Angeles for over 30 years and the tomahawk was among the street gangs as well. My friend Shark was with a group of new friends that invited him to a restaurant club on the weekend. This group was what many would consider the 'nerdy' group. Shortly after they arrived, there was a confrontation with these 'nerds' and some slightly intoxicated 'cool' guys over something meaningless, so one of the 'nerds' pulled out two compact tomahawks from of his back (under his jacket) and he was 'ready to rumble.' The 'cool' guys didn't feel so 'cool' anymore and ran outside to 'cool off.' At the Apache reservations I visited, most household had tomahawks in their living space. I spent a couple weeks at Firebase Chamkani when I lived in Afghanistan. A few weeks after I left this base, the local village across the street from the base brought in two family members that had just been attacked by the Taliban. The Taliban had taken a tomahawk and chopped the two men up and down, then left for dead because they had good relations with the US Army base. One man still had the tomahawk lodged into his spine which got stuck. He was pronounced dead on arrival (DOA).

The second man was still breathing. My buddy was there at the time. While the US Army medics were trying to save the 2nd guy, the DOA guy with the tomahawk in his back came back to life. They tried to keep him alive but he had lost too much blood and died a second time after a few minutes. I have heard many more tomahawk stories over the years and it does not surprise me to hear about them. Military troops in almost every country around the world still carry tomahawks or other wielding weapons in similar size. Learn what you can of the hawk. Learn its ways--for its ways are many. I carry one in my car, in my house, and in my studio. The hooking power and blunt force produced from a hawk can be fatal. Use only the force necessary in any situation. Avoid conflict as much as humanly possible but when no other options are available, you must use the hawk my friend—to serve and protect. I started researching Apache Knife Fighting & Battle Tactics from various Apache tribal members around 1993. I taught my first of many seminars on the topic in 1995 and I've been teaching since then. I learn more every year and continue to add to the Apache History books. Like the cunning Apache Raven, continue to learn from both the past and the present.

Enjoy your journey!

TABLE OF CONTENTS

INTRODUCTION   PAGE 9

SAFETY & USE OF FORCE   PAGE 13

NOMENCLATURE   PAGE 21

SELECTION   PAGE 23

GRIPS & GRIP SWITCHES   PAGE26

GUARDS, POSTURES & POSITIONS   PAGE 32

FOOTWORK   PAGE 44

DEFENSIVE TECHNIQUES   PAGE 54

OFFENSIVE TECHNIQUES   PAGE 68

ATTACK PATTERNS AND TEMPLATES   PAGE 85

ANATOMY & PHYSIOLOGY   PAGE 93

RECOMMENDED INSTRUCTORS   PAGE 107

BIBLIOGRAPHY   PAGE 108

INTRODUCTION

INTRODUCTION

Having trained in Native American blade craft, I cannot avoid being asked if this is a traditional Native American tomahawk system. The answer to that is a definite no. I have trained in knife arts of the Apache tradition and my instructor was always very clear that tomahawks were not traditional Apache weapons. The apaches would acquire them but they were not original to them. This system is the Way of the Raven Blade and Impact Weapons systems applied to the use of the Hawk. Our system is a distillation of Native American, European and Asian blade work combined with common sense research and development. Many things translate to the hawk and many things don't.

I am a huge proponent of playing to the strengths of any given weapon. I do not try to "force" techniques onto a weapon when they make no sense. I have observed various tomahawk systems being taught today. Many of them are traditional martial arts being applied to the hawk. This is in itself not a good thing or a bad thing. As I mentioned earlier, some movements and techniques are not applicable to every weapon. The hawk is a top heavy weapon whose strength lies in devastating strikes and chops using the weapons inertia. The Hawk is not a Kali stick. A kali stick is a weapon made from light rattan. It is evenly balanced. A kali stick can be manipulated with pin point precision and it can start and stop on a dime. I have observed classes teaching tomahawk as a kali stick. What I have also observed is that the instructors 99% of the time are using itty bitty baby hawks or very light hawk trainers. If you tried ½ of what they taught using my full tang battle ready steel hawk you would rip any number of ligaments and damage yourself much more than your enemy. Hawks come in different sizes and weights so this can vary from person to person and weapon to weapon.

When you look at the family the hawk comes from we are talking about hatchets, hammers, and small axes, it makes more sense to treat this weapon as what it is rather than pretending it is a stick or a sword. For this reason our system does not look as flashy or fancy as other systems out there. I was asked once to show how to disarm a knife wielding attacker with a tomahawk. I told the student that the dis-arm would be to literally chop through the freaking arm. There you go. DIS-ARM. That is our method and our approach. The axe is one of the earliest tools and weapons formed by man. Primitive axes can be traced back as far as the Stone Age. The axe is a primal tool linked to man's earliest existence. The tomahawk is just one such tool in this family of weapons which can be found in virtually every culture thought history and the world. The tomahawk was an indigenous weapon found in the Americas before European colonization. The word "tomahawk" is derived from the Algonquian words Tomahak or Tamahakan meaning "used for cutting". Early tomahawks were made with stone heads, which quickly evolved to metal after the Europeans brought new materials and technology to the Americas.

As a weapon the tomahawk was used by several Native American tribes such as the Algonquian, and the Sioux. The tomahawk quickly became popular with Europeans settlers for its versatility and effectiveness. In the 18th century, the Continental Congress of the United States in a resolution dated July 18, 1775, decreed that militiamen must provide themselves with a sword or Tomahawk in addition to muskets and bayonets.

Though not general issue, the tomahawk was carried into war by soldiers in both WWII and the Korean War. In the mid to late 1960's a Mohawk WWII veteran, Peter Lagana produced and sold battle ready hawks to soldiers fighting in the Vietnam War. Today the tomahawk has experienced a small revival in the military community. Tomahawks, while still not general issue items, can be found in campaigns in places such as Afghanistan and Iraq.

The versatility of the tomahawk has also begun to be accepted by law enforcement agencies. The tomahawk has made inroads into special operation units as a multipurpose breeching tool. The tomahawk is also the perfect weapon/tool for the outdoorsman in rural or semi-rural areas. The tomahawk does not seem to be an obvious civilian weapon for urban environments. If you think about it however, it makes for a great home defense weapon and fits nicely in any car.

SAFETY & USE OF FORCE

SAFETY IN TRAINING

Safety should be the paramount consideration during any training activity. We train so that we can protect ourselves and not get hurt. Why then would we allow being hurt in training? It is the responsibility of the instructor and all class participants to ensure the safety of all. All participants in a training activity should be led through a proper warm up and stretching routine before class begins.

SAFETY EQUIPMENT

Warriors should also use appropriate safety equipment for all training sessions. Equipment that should be used includes:

-Athletic Cup   -Forearm shields

-Athletic Mouth Piece   -Safety Goggles

-Safety head gear   -Safety Gloves

SAFETY TRAINING WEAPONS

Warriors should also use safe training weapons. A variety of training blades should be used from rubber to aluminum trainers. Dulled Live blades are inappropriate for anything but solo training purposes. NO LIVE WEAPONS SHOULD EVER BE ALLOWED IN THE TRAINING AREA. A good friend of mine was working in a seminar with another instructor. The Instructor drew his blade and cut my friend across the inside of his forearm as part of his demo. The only problem is that he drew his live blade and not a trainer.

Luckily a few stitches were all that were needed that day. I shudder to think what would have happened if the instructor would have been demonstrating a neck cut?

OTHER CONSIDERATIONS

-Training should be conducted in reasonable proximity of emergency medical care

-Training should be conducted in a designated training area with adequate flooring, padding and ventilation.

SAMPLE FORCE CONTINUUM

SUBJECT ACTION	WARRIOR RESPONSE
Cooperation	Verbal Commands
Passive Resistance	Escort Control
Active Resistance	Control & Compliance Holds
Assault Which Can Result in Bodily Harm	Defensive Tactics/Mechanical Controls/Less Lethal Weapons
Assault Which Can Result In Serious Bodily Harm or Death	Deadly Force

The use of force continuum presented is a general model based on common U.S. use of force guidelines. The continuum presented is for illustrative purposes only. Warriors or any other person utilizing the RAVEN Method is responsible for following all applicable local, state or federal laws.

FORCE CONTINUUM

The force continuum is a conceptual tool which exists to aid Warriors in determining what level of force is required and justified in controlling the actions of an assailant. Verbal commands, escort techniques, mechanical controls, and deadly force are all options which are available to a Warrior depending upon the assailants actions. Force escalation must cease when the assailant complies with the commands of the Warrior, and/or the situation is controlled by the Warrior. The model presented bellow consists of five levels. Physical defensive tactics are appropriate from levels three to five.

Level One: The assailant cooperates with the Warrior's verbal commands. Physical actions are not required.

Level Two: The assailant is unresponsive to verbal commands. Assailant cooperation however is achieved with escort techniques.

Level Three: The assailant actively resists the Warrior's attempts to control without being assault. Compliance and control holds as well as pain compliance techniques are appropriate actions at this time.

Level Four: The assailant assaults a Warrior or another person with actions which are likely to cause bodily harm. Appropriate action would include mechanical controls or defensive tactics such as stunning techniques. Impact and chemical weapons may be appropriate at this level.

Level Five: The assailant assaults a Warrior or another person with actions which are likely to cause serious bodily harm or death if not stopped immediately. Appropriate Warrior action would include deadly force through mechanical controls, Impact weapons or firearms. Deadly force should be considered only when lesser means have been exhausted, are unavailable or cannot be reasonably employed.

DECISION OF FORCE

When making the decision to use force a Warrior should use the minimal amount of "Reasonable" force necessary to safely control the situation at hand. When using deadly force for self defense a Warrior must be prepared to articulate and justify their use of a force. A blade should not be employed unless the Warrior has deemed the situation at hand to be a lethal force conflict devoid of reasonable access to escape.

"Reasonable force" can be defined: *force that is not excessive and is the least amount of force that will permit safe control of the situation while still maintaining a level of safety for himself or herself and the public.*

A Warrior is justified in the use of force when they reasonably believe it to be necessary to defend themselves or another from bodily harm and have no avenue for reasonable escape.

Escalation and de-escalation of resistance and response may occur without going through each successive level. The Warrior has the option to escalate or disengage, repeat the technique, or escalate to any level at any time. However, the Warrior will need to justify any response to resistance. If the Warrior skips levels, he or she must explain why it was necessary to do so.

TOTALITY OF CIRCUMSTANCES

Totality of circumstances refers to all facts and circumstances known to the Warrior at the time. The totality of circumstances includes consideration of the assailant's form of resistance, all reasonably perceived factors that may have an effect on the situation, and the response options available to the Warrior.

SAMPLE FACTORS MAY INCLUDE THE FOLLOWING:

- o Severity of the assault or battery
- o Assailant is an immediate threat
- o Assailant's mental or psychiatric history, if known to the Warrior
- o Assailant's violent history, if known to the Warrior
- o Assailant's combative skills
- o Assailant's access to weapons
- o Innocent bystanders who could be harmed
- o Number of assailant's vs. number of Warriors
- o Duration of confrontation

- Assailant's size, age, weight, and physical condition
- The Warrior's size, age, weight, physical condition, and defensive tactics expertise
- Environmental factors, such as physical terrain, weather conditions, etc.

In all cases where your assessment and decision are questioned you may need to demonstrate the following:

- That you felt physically threatened by and in danger from the suspect, i.e. that the suspect's behavior (body language/ words / actions) were aggressive and threatening;

- That you used force as a last resort, and that you used the reasonable amount;

- That you stopped using force once you had the suspect and the situation under control.

- That the Warrior has exhausted all reasonable efforts to escape the situation.

NOMENCLATURE

TOMAHAWK SELECTION & NOMENCLATURE
BY JAMES "OGRE" SMITH & FERNAN VARGAS

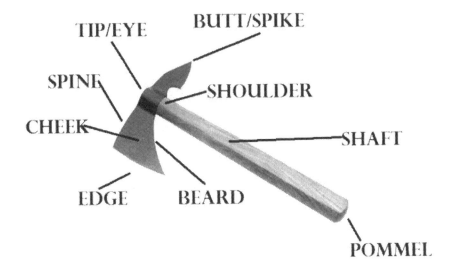

What are Hawk combatives without a Hawk? We obviously need to start here. Selecting the proper blade is a very individualized process. Every Warrior will have a different preference. There are however a few primary selling points on your shopping list. There are many things to think about when choose your Hawk. How are you going to use your Hawk? How are you going to carry your Hawk? How are you planning to deploy your Hawk?

TOMAHAWK SELECTION

GOOD GRIP

There is always talk of the quality of steel but I rarely hear talk about the quality of a grip. Master Peter Brusso helped me to appreciate the importance of a good grip. The blade can be made of adamantium, but if you can't hold onto your Hawk the blade is useless. The grip should feel good to you and not feel too big or too small.

GOOD STEEL

The steel of the Hawk is what make it good or bad. The minimum steel that I would choose would be 440 stainless. I would choose the best steel I could get within my budget. Remember that this Hawk could save your life or the life of someone else. Good choices in steels would be ATS-34, CPV440, 154CM, AUS8, and VG-10. This short list is far from all of the great steels on the market.

CORRECT EDGE TYPE AND GRIND

Be sure you choose the correct edge and grind for what you will be cutting. A hollow ground or fine V grind edge is great at cutting but is not as strong as a convex or a wider V grind. If you are in areas where you cannot risk your blade breaking (military or in the wilderness) you would choose the heavier grind and larger blade.

SO WHICH HAWKS DO WE RECOMMEND?

My recommendation in factory made Hawks is the Cold Steel Company. Over the years hundreds of people have asked me for my opinion on various blade products. My opinion has never changed.

When it comes to dollar for dollar value it is almost impossible to beat a Cold Steel Hawk in terms of quality or variety of selection. Cold Steel Hawks are well built, safe for the user and Cold steel also offers a huge selection of blades from tactical folders to military combat Hawks including non-metallic Hawks.

GRIPS & GRIP SWITCHES

DRAWING METHODS

A Weapon is only as good as how accessible it is. All training
exercises should begin with the Warrior drawing their hawk. Hawks
are not as concealable as knives, and because of their size there are
only a few logical places to carry one. The two primary ways to carry
a hawk are on the hip or over the shoulder. Both of these carry
positions offer quick deployment and do not cause significant
diminishment of mobility. Most commercially available hawks come
with a very basic sheath if any at all. I highly recommend that
individuals spend the extra money for a custom carry rig. Smaller
hawks may be better suited for over the shoulder carry than larger
ones.

SINGLE HANDED GRIPS: THE LONG GRIP

The Forward grip is executed by taking the hawk in the hand in a firm yet relaxed manner. The hand will form a fist around the handle with the thumb resting on the index finger. The edge of the blade should be facing away from the Warrior and in alignment with the Warriors middle knuckle line tip up to the sky. Many instructors will advocate a modified version of this grip, often called a saber grip. In the saber grip the Warrior's thumb will rest on the spine of the blade. While this gives additional support through strong skeletal alignment, I do not recommend this grip. The reason being that a strong "blade beat", or even inadvertent jamming can easily dislodge the weapon. If this grip is used it should be done so sparingly once the Warrior is in the midst of an attack. It should also be noted that the stripping defense methods found in south East Asian martial arts are often less effective against the Heaven grip. The Heaven grip should be used when maximum range is desired as it allows the Warrior to more effectively work from the long range.

TWO HANDED GRIPS: THE AXE GRIP

The axe grip is executed by taking the hawk in two hands in a manner similar to the long grip. The hands will rest low on the shaft in a firm yet relaxed manner. The edge of the blade should be facing away from the Warrior. The axe grip is most useful for extremely powerful attacks and blocks.

GRIP CHANGE: PALMING

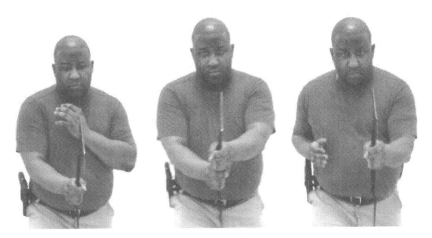

In order to use a Palming grip change the Warrior will bring their hawk to their center line. Once at center line the live hand will open and will meet the weapon hand, covering it. As this is occurring, the rear leg will step up to the same depth as the lead leg. At this point the Warrior will pass the blade from one hand to the other. Once the hawk has switched hands, the former lead leg will fall to the back so that the lead leg will match the weapon hand.

GRIP CHANGE: HIDDEN PALM

The Hidden palm switch is executed as a tactical maneuver. The Warrior with the hawk in their dominant hand will turn their body to the inside so that the shoulder and dominant side of the body obscure the enemy's line of site to the non-dominant side. As the Warrior turns they will switch the hawk from the dominant hand to the non-dominant hand. The Warrior will then uncoil and execute a thrust with the non-dominant hand.

GUARDS, POSTURES & POSITIONS

HAND POSITIONING

Camillo Agrippa was an Italian Mathematician, engineer and architect who wrote Tratto Di Scienzia d'Armes, a Rapier fencing manual studied widely to this day. Agrippa was the first to present and break down the four hand positions used by almost every fencer since. The hand positions in fencing are directly related to the guards based on the quadrant concept. Each is used in conjunction with a guard in order to cover the four quadrants of the body. This is also the case in our system. While we use more guards than the classic four, our additional guards come only from how we choose to categorize the variations in elevation of the hand and are essentially the same as those taught by Agrippa. The four hand positions are: Prima (first), Seconda (second), Terz (third), Quarta (fourth).

Larry Tom, in the article Hand Work for the Dueling Sword explains that;

"The hand positions relate directly to the guards, each of which protects one of the four quadrants. Once you assume one of the guards, you have closed that quadrant off from your opponent's attack, leaving the other three quadrants vulnerable to an attack. Because you are aware that the guard in which you position yourself only protects you in that one quadrant, you are "inviting" your opponent to attack in one of the other quadrants. The key in the invitation is to anticipate and even direct your opponent's attack so that you in turn can successfully defend and counterattack. "

PRIMA

In Prima your palm will be facing to the outside and your thumb will be pointing downward on a vertical line. Prima is used to cover the low inside quadrant. The natural thrusting line for Prima is inward. The Prima hand position lends itself to overhead guards. Guards using Prima will offer excellent protection to the upper parts of the body.

SECONDA

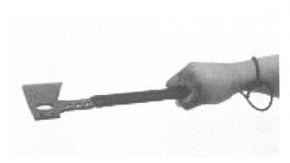

In Seconda your palm will be facing downwards to the floor and your thumb will be pointing to the left. Seconda is used to cover the low outside quadrant. The natural thrusting line for Seconda is from outside to inside. The Seconda hand position lends itself to outside guards. Seconda protects the upper body almost as well as Prima.

TERZA

In Terza your palm will be facing left and your thumb will be pointing upwards on a vertical line. Terza is used to cover the high outside quadrant. The natural thrusting line for Terza is straight in. The Terza hand position lends itself to guards down the centerline of the body. This hand position is the most commonly used. Terza is used in the primary stance and guard of the system. Terza allows for easy transition to seconda and Quarta.

QUARTA

In Quarta your palm will be facing upwards and your thumb will be pointing to the right. Quarta is used to cover the high inside quadrant. The natural thrusting line for Quarta is inside to outside. The Quarta hand position lends itself to inside guards. Quarta is excellent for protecting the inside line of the body.

THE NINE WARDS

In the Way of the Raven System there are several Guard positions that the Warrior can assume. The primary default guard of the system is the center middle guard adopted from the "warrior stance". This Primary guard offers good options to the Warrior. From this guard the Warrior has facility for both defense and attack. The eight secondary guards are postures which the Warrior will find themselves in temporarily after an attack or defense motion. The Eight secondary guards can also be used by the seasoned Warrior to invite certain attacks or responses from the enemy. An inside middle guard for example invites a high attack on the Warrior's dominant side. The Warrior can use this to their advantage. The Warrior invites the attack by using a certain guard in order to pounce with a well-planned and timed counter attack. Keep in mind that these wards may be adopted as initial postures or the Warrior may find themselves in any given ward as a way adopting a defensive posture at any given point within a movement. For example, a Warrior may execute a horizontal cut from right to left and find themselves in the "Inside Middle Guard" at the end of their action. A Warrior may find themselves purposefully holding a guard for an extended period of time or they may hold it only briefly while in transition.

CENTER HIGH GUARD

The Center high guard is achieved by holding the hawk slightly
overhead at the Warrior's center line. The hawk hand will extend
outward away from the Warrior approximately 12 inches. The hand
will be in a thumb down position. The eye of the hawk is facing the
enemy.

CENTER MIDDLE GUARD

The Center Middle Guard is achieved by holding the hawk slightly above the naval at the Warrior's center line. The eye of the hawk will be canted at a 45 degree angle towards the enemy.

CENTER LOW GUARD

The Center Low Guard is achieved by holding the hawk slightly underneath the naval at the Warrior's center line. The eye of the hawk will be canted at a 45 degree angle towards the enemy.

HIGH OUTSIDE GUARD

The high outside guard is achieved by holding the hawk palm down in front of the Warrior and to the outside of the body approximately 12 inches. The hawk hand will be held the approximate elevation of the Warrior's temple. The point of the hawk is facing the enemy.

MIDDLE OUTSIDE GUARD

The Middle outside guard is achieved by holding the hawk palm down in front of the Warrior and to the outside of the body approximately 12 inches. The weapon hand will be held the approximate \elevation of the Warrior's diaphragm. The eye of the hawk is facing the enemy.

LOW OUTSIDE GUARD

The low outside guard is achieved by holding the blade palm facing inside (thumb up) in front of the Warrior and to the outside of the body approximately 12 inches. The weapon hand will be held the approximate elevation of the Warrior's hip or waist. The eye of the hawk is facing the enemy.

HIGH INSIDE GUARD

The high inside guard is achieved by holding the blade palm up in front of the Warrior and to the inside of the body approximately 12 inches. The weapon hand will be held the approximate elevation of the Warrior's temple. The eye of the hawk is facing the enemy. * In the reverse grip the hand will be held so that the bottom of the fist is facing the attacker.

MIDDLE INSIDE GUARD

The Middle inside guard is achieved by holding the blade palm up in front of the Warrior and to the inside of the body approximately 12 inches from the center line. The weapon hand will be held the approximate elevation of the Warrior's diaphragm. The eye of the hawk is facing the enemy.

LOW INSIDE GUARD

The low inside guard is achieved by holding the blade palm up in front of the Warrior and to the inside of the body approximately 12 inches. The weapon hand will be held the approximate elevation of the Warrior's hip or waist. The eye of the hawk is facing the enemy.

THE WARRIOR STANCE

The warrior stance is taken by standing Square with the feet approximately 12 inches apart. The Warrior will then take their non-dominant leg and slide it back about 10 inches. The dominant leg will have the foot planted firmly on the ground. The non-dominant leg will be planted on the ball of the foot. The knees should be slightly bent. The hips and shoulders should be in alignment. The torso will be upright, do not crouch. The weapon hand will be held in front of the body at center line. The elbow should be bent with the eye of the hawk facing the opponent. It is crucial when adopting this posture that the Warrior keep their entire body behind their extended Hawk. No part of the body should be flush with the Hawk or in front of it. The extended Hawk should be thought of as a shield.

If the enemy wishes to attack any part of the Warrior's body they must first contend with the Hawk. Much is made about blading the body for target denial. We feel this is a mistake in blade fighting. One of the key reasons a Warrior would blade their body is to establish a structure that is bio-mechanically correct for executing blows and strikes. In weapon fighting the blade does most of the work and we need not adopt a bladed stance in order to deliver effective blows. Also, it is important to note that a bladed body is much easier to flank than a body in the warrior stance.

THE COMMANDO STANCE

The Commando stance presented here is a slight variation of the stance taught throughout WWII by such combative luminaries as William Fairbairn and Rex Applegate. The stance varies from the original taught in WWII. The lead arm is held vertically not horizontal. Man is a vertical animal. Eyes, throat, heart, etc basically run down the center line of the body. The vertical lead arm can help shield these targets better than if it is held horizontal. The posture is taken by blading the body at a 45 degree angle, the hawk is held closely to the rear with the live hand in front guarding the body's center line in a vertical position. This stance is used only against unarmed enemies or as a baiting tactic. A Warrior should never take this posture when facing another similarly armed enemy. There are several reasons for this. First, an unarmed enemy is likely to focus on immobilizing the Warrior's Hawk. By keeping the Hawk to the rear, the Live Hand is able to act as an obstacle to this goal by striking, parrying, and redirecting the enemy. The second reason why this stance should be adopted only against unarmed enemies is that while the live hand can be very useful against an unarmed foe it is an easy target against a Hawk. When the Warrior blades their body and keeps the live hand in front as a vertical shield, the Warrior is properly preparing to deal with an empty hand assailant. The bladed body structure and live hand to the front give the Warrior good bio-mechanical structure to deal with incoming blows. Against an edged weapon attack this structure would be more or a liability than an advantage.

KNEE STANCE

The Backward Stance should be executed by bringing the weapon hand back close the rib cage, and placing the free hand vertically in front of the body. The body should be very bladed and in line with the free hand. The Warrior should also take one knee is able as it allows more mobility than two This stance is advocated for use when the Warrior has

been knocked down or has fallen and must defend themselves before being able to recover to a standing position. The weapon is held back so that the Warrior can use the free hand to block or deflect blows and kicks.

FOOT WORK

ABOUT FOOT WORK

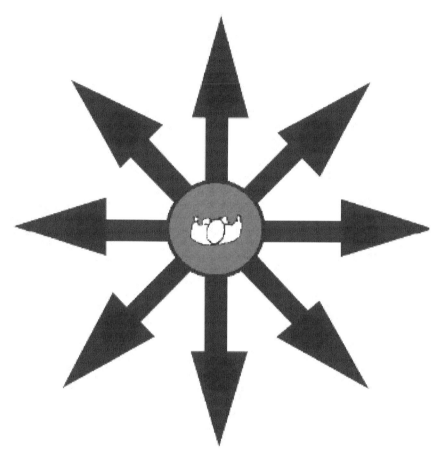

For the Warrior, good footwork is paramount. There is arguably no aspect of the fighting arts more important than footwork. The Warrior will be well served to develop through drill and practice, flowing and quick footwork. More important however than speed is precision. The foot work of the Warrior must be precise in both offensive and defensive actions in order to ensure success. A Warrior can use good foot work to help control the scenario and maintain an advantage. Lack of proper foot work will make victory nearly impossible for the

Warrior. Proper foot work however can help to offset other weaknesses in a Warrior's repertoire. In any encounter a Warrior can use linear movement both forward and backwards, diagonal movement (45 degrees) forward or backwards, and horizontal movement from side to side. It is crucial that the Warrior learn to move smoothly in every direction, both on the advance and the retreat. Whenever the Warrior initiates an attack they should initially seek to identify the angle which will offer least resistance to their attack. By capitalizing on the least defended angle the Warrior improves their odds of successfully completing their attack. This means that the Warrior should attack on an open line, or attack after proactively opening an enemy's line. When on the defensive, the Warrior should seek to identify the angle which is absent of aggressive force, in doing so the Warrior rather than clashing with the enemy will simply evade or escape.

THE ADVANCE

To Advance, refers to any time the Warrior takes steps towards the Enemy. The goal of any Warrior is to always attempt to establish proper distance from the enemy which places the Warrior in a position of advantage. There are times in which advancing steps are necessary to accomplish this. A Warrior may therefore advance to gain the proper range to complete an attack or to jam or pass an enemy

THE RETIRE

To retire refers to any time the Warrior takes steps away from the Enemy. The goal of any Warrior is to always attempt to establish proper distance from the enemy which places the Warrior in a position of advantage. There are times in which retreating steps are necessary to accomplish this. A Warrior may therefore retire after making a successful attack in order to be at a safer distance.

WARRIOR WALKING

Warrior walking is just what the name implies. It is walking, a natural foot over foot way of walking. Like most people in the martial arts I was first taught how to "Properly" move, step and slide, step and shuffle etc. It was not until I met Mescalero Apache Knife instructor Mr. Lopez that I learned the value of just naturally walking. In his family system of knife work Lopez advocates natural walking because it is faster, more fluid and more natural than a shuffle step. At first analysis I thought it was a flawed idea. Upon applying natural walking in practice and sparring my teachers lesson was confirmed. The Natural step allowed me to move with greater fluidity.

FORWARD TRIANGLE: THE MONKEY EVASION

The Warrior will use a triangular footwork pattern to move toward the subject and inside the weapon's arc of danger. The Warrior begins by standing with the feet together on the tip of an imaginary triangle or the bottom of an imaginary "V". In the Silat combatives system of Pukulan Penchat Silat Tempur this evasion is known as the Monkey Evasion.

MOVING TO THE RIGHT

While picturing an assailant standing in front of the Warrior he or she will take a moderate step forward on a 45 degree angle to the right with the right foot. The back or left foot will remain stationary or will shuffle forward slightly.

MOVING TO THE LEFT

While picturing an assailant standing in front of the Warrior he or she will take a moderate step forward on a 45 degree angle to the left with the left foot. The back or right foot will remain stationary or will shuffle forward slightly. This simple stepping pattern allows us to move off-line of the attack, inside the arc of danger while still allowing us to move into the assailant for follow-up control.

REVERSE TRIANGLE: MONKEY EVASION

The reverse triangle is the reverse of the female triangle. In this pattern the Warrior will move backwards on a 45 degree angle.

MOVING TO THE RIGHT

While picturing an assailant standing in front of the Warrior he or she will take a moderate step backwards on a 45 degree angle to the right with the right foot. The back or left foot will remain stationary or will shuffle forward slightly.

MOVING TO THE LEFT

While picturing an assailant standing in front of the Warrior he or she will take a moderate step backwards on a 45 degree angle to the left with the left foot. The back or right foot will remain stationary or will shuffle forward slightly.

FORWARD PIVOT: SNAKE EVASION

The forward pivot is performed by turning on the ball of your lead foot while simultaneously swinging your rear leg forward in front of you. In the Silat combatives system of Pukulan Penchat Silat Tempur this evasion is known as the Snake Evasion

REAR PIVOT: SNAKE EVASION

The rear pivot is executed by turning on the ball of the rear foot while simultaneously swinging your lead leg to the back.

LATERAL EVASION: TIGER EVASION

The lateral evasion is performed by stepping quickly to the right or the left. If stepping right, step your right foot out first then bring your left over and assume a well-balanced posture. When stepping left, step your left foot out first and then bring your right over and assume a well-balanced posture. In the Silat combatives system of Pukulan Penchat Silat Tempur this evasion is known as the Tiger Evasion.

LUNGE

In order to perform a correct lunge step the Warrior should take a small step forward with the toes up. The lead leg will bend bringing the knee forward. The Warrior should take care that the front knee be just above the front instep of the lead leg. Bending the knee further could take the Warrior off balance, while too shallow a bend will cause the Warrior to take an ineffective posture. The rear leg will be at full extension with the rear foot flat on the floor while the free hand swings to the rear for counter balance.

INTIGLIATA

The intigliata is a step taken by the lead leg to the opposite side at a 45 degree angle forwards. The step is used to evade by removing the outside target.

CHECK STEP

In Essentials of Fencing Technique, Richard Howard explains that a "Check step is an effective way to confuse the tactical thinking of an opponent." There in effect, two distinct check steps. In the first the Warrior will indicate an advance by taking a half step forward with the lead leg but does not move the rear leg. The Warrior will then quickly take a full step back. In the second the Warrior will indicate a retreat by taking a half step back with the rear leg but does not move the lead leg. The Warrior will then quickly take a full step forward.

DEFENSIVE TECHNIQUES

VOIDING THE BODY

"I was an on duty EMT responding to a call. Everything seemed like a medical call when we came through the door but moments into our evaluation things went south. As I attempted to reach down for my blood pressure cuff the young man jumped up and grabbed a full sized kitchen knife off the cluttered counter and swiped at my face. I jerked my head back, as the blade passed by my face, then I hollowed out at the core when the blade swept back across the path that would have been my gut. "

-Master Jesse Lawn

This story was recounted to me during my research by American Ninjutsu Master Jesse Lawn. Master Lawn successfully used the defensive concept of voiding the body to protect himself against an emotionally disturbed patient who made serious efforts to kill him. Master Lawn's account clearly illustrates the "Sway" and "Deer" techniques as taught in the Way of the Raven System. Both techniques are based on instinctive body reaction; this is one of the reasons why they are so effective. They fine-tuned variations of a movement that the body wishes to do instinctively when in danger. In the world of warriors there is an old adage, "The best defense is not being there." We hold this adage to be true and it is a corner stone of our defensive maneuvers and philosophy. While checking hands and blocking techniques are a necessary part of any Warrior's repertoire, I would like to pay special attention to the art of voiding the body as a means of defense. In this chapter we will be looking at the defensive concept of "Voiding the body". In the Way of the Raven System Voiding the body takes a more prevalent role in defense than blocking or checking. Voiding the body is simply explained as such. When the enemy attacks any part of the Warrior's anatomy, the Warrior will remove said target from area of attack, thus protecting it from harm. This is done in a number of ways. In his writings Fencing author Capo Ferro suggests that a good fighter will always follow up a parry or a voiding of the body with a counter attack.

TO VOID OR TO CHECK, THAT IS THE QUESTION......

The majority of the blade work I see in other schools and through video media is extremely reliant on the use of the checking hand. There are various drills that are popular training tools. These drills make their practitioners very good at checking. The level of hand speed and coordination is greatly augmented by these drills. At first glance it seems like a pretty effective way of training. It was not until I began training in the European and American Arts that I began to truly see the use of foot work and body voids as a means of effective defense. One of my instructors, Guru Brandt Smith once told me not to be lazy. He explained to me that foot work and body voids were essential to my defense. It wasn't until I was able to properly use footwork and body voids that Guru Brandt introduced the checking hands. I had a similar experience with Mr. Lopez. Blocking was not frowned upon, but if you could defend with movement, you were expected to. Interestingly this concept is not limited to blade work.

The famous Bare-knuckle Boxer Mendoza also advocated voiding the body over using parries. I reflect back on Guru Brandt telling me not to be lazy. Laziness? Yes, he was right. I see it all the time. You see, you can get away with using bad foot work or under developed foot work without too many negative consequences if you're able to use the checking hand to compensate. This is a real problem. I personally feel much more comfortable using movement to defend myself. In spite of my personal preference I see the need to train both aspects of defense. I therefore go on the record with this statement. If you are using the checking hand to compensate for your footwork/body movement you are training incorrectly. Instead you should be using your checking hands to complement your footwork/body movement. This implies that you have developed both skills to the correct level and use them at the appropriate time and under the appropriate circumstances. If I am fighting in an open parking lot then I should be using movement as my primary defense. If I take a good cut to the checking hand to the point that it is disabled, using it may be a moot point. I may have no choice but to use foot work. Similarly, what if I am in a narrow corridor, or between parked cars? What If I have taken a disabling cut to the leg(s)? Foot work may not be an option and I sure as hell better know how to use that checking hand.

THE SWAY

When an attack comes at a high line, the Warrior simply throws their shoulders backwards taking the head outside the arc of danger. The Warrior will pull their chin to their chest and bring their hands under their chin while shrugging the shoulders. This combination of movement offers the Warrior the greatest amount of protection. By tucking the chin and shrugging the shoulders the Warrior is "shielding the carotid arteries. Bringing in the hands close under the chin keeps the hands from remaining out in the open where they can easily be cut.

DEER TECHNIQUE

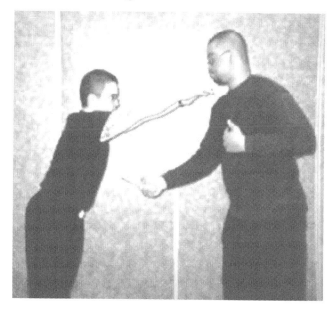

When an attack comes at a low line, the Warrior will hollow out their abdomen and throw their hips and buttocks backwards taking the torso outside the arc of danger. The Warrior's back will curl like a letter "C" allowing the hands will to come forward as a counter balance, and possible attack. In both cases the hands come up as a counter balance and more importantly to protect the vital areas.

REASSEMBLEMENT

The reassemblement is the action of withdrawing the lead leg to the rear either to or past the rear leg. The reassemblement is used as a defensive technique as it voids the leg from possible attack. The final posture of the movement closely resembles the "Deer" defensive technique.

THE DUCK

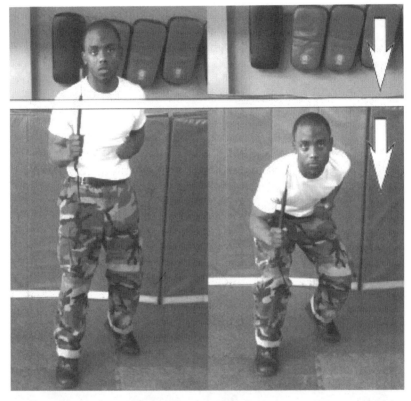

There are times when the best defense for a Warrior is to drop their level in order to avoid an attack to the high line. To execute a duck the Warrior must lower their level. This is achieved not by bending at the waist or lowering the head by bending the neck but by bending the legs while keeping the back and neck straight. This is done so that the Warrior can keep their eyes on the enemy at all times.

60

THE SLIP

The Slip is an evasive movement of the head used to avoid incoming linear attacks. Just as in boxing, the Warrior will move their head and shoulders off line as to evade the attack. One trick taught to me by the Gallo Negro was to imagine throwing your shoulder at the incoming attack. This naturally creates the body mechanics needed to execute the movement correctly

VOIDING THE HAND

To defend both the weapon hand and the live hand the Warrior will "pull" the hand from the trajectory of the oncoming strike of the enemy. The Warrior can use the movement hand movement patterns in order to achieve this.

BLOCKING:

The Tomahawk offers great defensive capabilities to the Warrior. Because the hawk can be gripped in so many ways and has various striking surfaces, it offers a variety of defensive techniques. Despite the surface used, the Warrior will become accustomed to blocking in the four cardinal directions. Those directions are Up, Down, Right, Left or North, South, East, and West. Additionally, some grips offer slight variations to address the elevation of the attack. Presented here are five primary defensive sets and several other variations.

BLOCKS FROM THE LONG GRIP USING THE CHEEK

In this blocking series, the Warrior will be using the long grip. The Warrior will extend their hawk outwards to meet the incoming attack in a sweeping fashion. . The Warrior will use the cheek of the Hawk to strike into the in-coming attack.

BLOCKS FROM THE LONG GRIP USING THE HEAD

In this blocking series, the Warrior will be using the long grip. The Warrior will extend their hawk outwards to meet the incoming attack. The Warrior will receive the blow on the head of their hawk. The Warrior will basically thrust into the on-coming attack with the head of their weapon.

ONE HANDED BLOCKS

FROM THE LONG GRIP USING THE SHAFT

In photos one, two, three and six the Warrior will extend their hawk outwards to meet the incoming attack. The Warrior will receive the blow on the shaft of their hawk. In photo four and five the Warrior will adjust the hawk and cover with the live hand.

ROOF BLOCK

The Roof blocks are two blocks which are used to cover the right and the left side of the body protecting the head and neck. It is so named because the forearm and the weapon form a frame similar to the roof of a house. The blade is held at a right angle to the forearm, and the gripping hand is over the head. The blade faces in the blocking direction. To execute the inside roof block the Warrior will raise their weapon hand as if executing an empty hand upward block. The Warrior's head will be in between their arm and their weapon which will be pointing tip down. The strike of the enemy will land on the Warrior's weapon. The Warrior should step on a 45 degree angle away from their weapon so that the enemy's strike glances instead of hitting with full force.

To execute the outside roof block (often called a wing block) the Warrior will raise their elbow so that their weapon hand goes to the rear and the eye of the weapon points downward. Some choose to rest the weapon onto the arm/shoulder closest to it. The Warrior's arm and weapon should form the shape of an "A" on the outside of the Warrior's body. The strike of the enemy will land on the Warrior's weapon. The Warrior should step on a 45 degree angle away from their weapon so that the enemy's strike glances instead of hitting with full force.

SWEEPING BLOCK

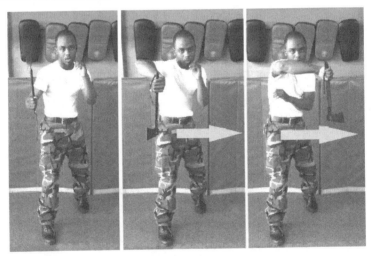

To execute the sweeping block the Warrior will drop the point of their weapon towards the floor from the outside of their body and then sweep across to the inside. This defense is used primarily against a foreword thrust to the midsection.

LIVE HAND PARRY

HIGH PARRY   **MIDDLE PARRY**   **LOW PARRY**

The live hand is used to block and parry attacks. In order to use the live hand for defense the Warrior will use an open hand to slap, or push the oncoming attack of the enemy. A parrying motion should be short and crisp. A Warrior should not over extend their body when executing the parry. The goal of the parry is not to be an obstacle to the enemy's attack but rather to deviate its trajectory away from its target by altering its course. The parry can be used effectively pushing an attack to the inside, to the outside, and downward.

OFFENSIVE TECHNIQUES

OFFENSIVE TECHNIQUES

In this section we will examine the various offensive techniques used in the system. It is important to note that there are several variations of the techniques presented. Only the core techniques will be presented here. The Warrior should practice all of these techniques and become proficient and comfortable with their execution.

CHEEK OR FLAT STRIKE

To execute the Flat Strike the Warrior will swing their hawk and make contact with the cheek or flat of the hawk. The Warrior is basically "slapping" with this striking surface. This attack can be done from virtually any direction, either forehand or backhand.

ONE HANDED CHOP

The one handed chop is executed from the long grip. The chop is a heavy cleaving blow. The chop can be executed with full follow through or by making contact and then rapidly retracting. It must be noted that the chop is just that. A chop. It is not a cut. A "cut" is an awkward and unlikely attack from the long grip.

BUTT STRIKE

To execute the Butt Strike the Warrior will swing their hawk and make contact with the back of the weapon or the butt of the hawk. This attack can be done from virtually any direction, either forehand or backhand.

TWO HANDED CHOP

The two handed chop is executed from the long grip. The chop is a heavy cleaving blow, delivered in a linear, not circular fashion. The two handed chop should only ever be executed with full power. Due to the fact that the blow is very telegraphed it should be used only as a final blow in a larger sequence.

THE THRUST

To execute the thrust the attack should begin from the chosen guard and extend outwards towards the target for the thrust and then return to the chosen guard with the point of the hawk oriented towards the enemy. A committed thrust should be made with complete follow through, bringing one's mass with them. When making a non-committed thrust the Warrior should move their hawk out and back rapidly like a piston.

ARM EXTENSION VS BODY EXTENSION

The thrust can be performed in two ways. The first is by simply extending the arm. The second is performed by extending the arm and expanding the body. This expansion is achieved by extending the blade arm forward while simultaneously pulling the live hand to the rear of the body. This motion will expand the Warrior's chest. The motion is similar to drawing a bow and arrow.

THE FOUR CARDINAL DIRECTIONS OF THE THRUST

There are four categories of thrust based on the area from which the attack originates and hand position.

1) The Imbroccata is a vertical descending thrust.

2) The Mandritta (Punta Mandritta) is a thrust coming from the outside of the body to the inside of the body.

3) The Roversa (Punta Roversa) is a thrust coming from the inside of the body to the outside of the body

4) The Stoccata is an ascending vertical thrust

THE ANGLE OF THE THRUST

Fencing master Puck Curtis in his article "Spanish Fencing notation Part 3: Fighting Distance" explains to us that Spanish fencing master Carranza in his work identifies the Right Angle as providing us with the best reach. If the hand is elevated, the angle becomes obtuse. If the hand is lowered the angle becomes Acute. Both the obtuse and acute angles have less reach than the right angle.

THE LUNGE

To perform a lunge attack the Warrior will extend the weapon arm until it is slightly higher than the shoulder. The lead leg will bend bringing the knee forward. Ideally the Warrior should have their front knee just above the instep of the leading foot. The rear leg will be at full extension with the rear foot flat on the floor while the free hand swings to the rear for counter balance.

STANDING LUNGE

The standing lunge differs slightly from the traditional lunge. To execute the standing lunge the Warrior must extend the blade arm and then shift their weight forward over the dominant leg while straightening the real leg. The movement is not as committed or dramatic as the traditional lunge. The Warrior will find that their foot placement is not nearly as wide as in a standard lunge. *Note: the live hand is thrown back in the photos to illustrate the classic execution of the technique. In combat it is advised that the live hand be kept close to the chest.

REAR LEG LUNGE OR REVERSE LUNGE

The rear leg lunge is virtually identical to a standard lunge with two exceptions. To execute the rear leg lunge the Warrior will begin from guard position. The Warrior will bring their lead leg back while extending their blade arm to attack. The Warrior is in effect lunging on their non-dominant side. The Warrior may also keep the live hand forward rather than backwards as in a traditional lunge.

DOWNWARD WIND

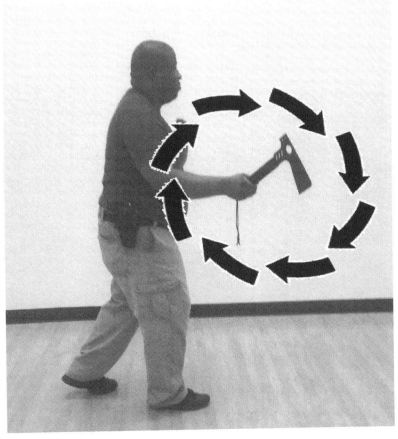

The downward wind is a cutting motion made by rotating the hawk clockwise into a downward cut. The rotation is made from the elbow, not the shoulder. The downward wind is usually executed in twos. Like the "Steel Wheel" the downward wind can be used in rapid succession for defense. The extended blade should be thought of as a shield. If the enemy wishes to reach any part of the Warrior's body they must first contend with the blade.

UPWARD WIND

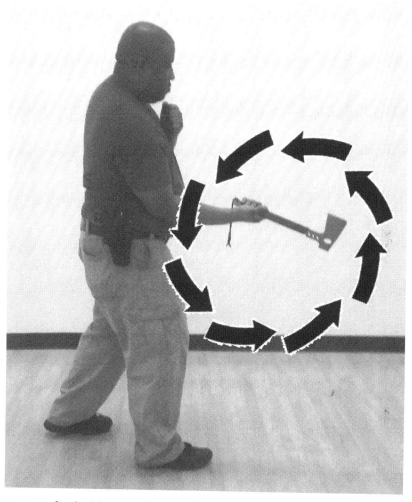

The upward wind is a cutting motion made by rotating the blade counter clockwise into an upward cut. The rotation is made from the elbow, not the shoulder. The downward wind is usually executed in twos. Like the "Steel Wheel" the downward wind can be used in rapid succession for defense. The extended blade should be thought of as a shield. If the enemy wishes to reach any part of the Warrior's body they must first contend with the blade.

BACK CUT

The back cut is a circular motion which utilized the false edge of the hawk. The Warrior can utilize the back cut from the outside of the body to the inside or from the inside of the body to the outside. The motion from either side is a swooping circular motion using the false edge or spine of the hawk as the point of impact. The inside to outside back cut is also extremely effective as a parrying motion.

AXING

Axing is a fully committed power cut. The Warrior will begin by stepping through with the strong side leg and simultaneously drop the blade from the high position down into their target. As the blade makes contact, the Warrior will sink into a deep horse stance allowing their entire body weight to pull through in the attack. At the end of the attack the Warrior will allow their attacking forearm to make contact with their thigh. This contact will prevent injury by preventing the Warrior from cutting into their leg.

POMMEL STRIKE

Pommel Strike. The pommel strike is executed by striking with the bottom of the hawk in a hammering motion.

NATURAL BODY WEAPONS

The Warrior should not become fixated on their hawk as the only weapon they have. If the opportunity presents its self, mechanical stunning techniques should also be used.

FALSE ATTACK

A false attack is a feint. Capo Ferro calls feints "those deceitful gestures of the sword" It is an attack that is never concerned with actually making contact with the enemy. The false attack is used for several reasons which include:

-To read his response to certain attacks

-To gauge the enemy's attributes such as quickness or reach

-To lure the enemy by eliciting a certain response, such as drawing their guard away to which the Warrior will have a planned attack.

–To disrupt the enemy's rhythm or momentum.

When executing a feint it is most common to feint in one direction and then attack the opposite. That is if the Warrior feints high he will then attack low, if he feints left then he will attack right. This is not required but it is the most common way of utilizing the feint before an attack.

MEYER'S DECEPTION

German combat master Joachim Meyer advocated a method of deceiving the enemy in his writings where the Warrior would change cuts to thrusts and thrusts to cuts. In his works Meyer explains that the initial attack should be extended out towards the enemy half way and when the enemy begins to enact their defense, the Warrior will change trajectory around the defense and change the nature of the attack from cut to thrust or from thrust to cut thus deceiving the enemy.

STOP THRUST

The stop thrust is made as the enemy is preparing to attack. It is used to intercept the enemy's motion. The stop thrust must be well timed. The Warrior must be able to anticipate or react quickly to the signs of motion that the enemy gives away. The stop thrust is exceptionally useful in stopping the enemy's forward momentum.

RIPOSTE

A Riposte is a counter offensive action. A riposte is an attack that is delivered immediately after parrying an attack from the enemy. A riposte usually travels in the same line opened by the parry and is distinguished by the fact that the Warrior does not re-set to their guard position after the parry and then initiate an attack, as that would be defined as a "*Reprise*". In traditional swordplay the parry which occurs prior to a counter attack is performed by making contact between the Warrior's blade and the enemy's blade. In mixed blade fighting, blade on blade contact may or may not be an option depending on the length of the blades in play. For our purposes a parry made with the body rather than the blade (such as the forearm) which is immediately followed by an attack is still considered a riposte.

REPRISE

Unlike a *Riposte*, where a Warrior returns an attack immediately following a parry, the reprise is a new attack that is launched after the Warrior re-sets into a Guard position.

REMISE

When a Warrior makes an initial attack and then makes a secondary attack that follows the primary offensive maneuver without retracting their arm, it is referred to as a remise.

THE REDOUBLE.

Redoubling can be described as a renewed attack after an initial attack has been parried. If the enemy parries the Warrior's attack and fails to riposte the Warrior can now re-initiate their attack. The Warrior's attack should be quick and occur before the enemy resets to a protective guard.

Tomahawk Expert Raven Cain

ATTACK PATTERNS AND TEMPLATES

CUTTING PATTERNS

In the art of the blade there is arguably nothing more important than understanding how to effectively move the hawk in slash and thrust action. In our art we use a variety of cutting patterns to teach students the correct lines of attack, fluid motion, and overall comfort in manipulating the blade. Presented are several patterns. While it will be useful to the Warrior to learn and master all of them, mastery of even one will help the Warrior in developing their skill. Various patterns are presented so that the Warrior can break monotony in their training. The Warrior should aim for thousands of repetitions with a focus on correct form while mastering the patterns. Speed and power will come as a result of having proper technique. As the old USMC adage states, "Slow is smooth, and smooth is fast". All of the Cut & Thrust patterns should be drilled in the following variations:

STATIC: STANDING

In the beginning of a Warrior's training journey the Warrior should practice each Cut & Thrust pattern from 1. Each stance, 2. Each ward, 3. Each Grip, outlined in the system. When using the Cut & Thrust patterns in a static drill the Warrior should stand in one place and execute each movement in the pattern selected. The Warrior should begin slowly and then gradually increase their speed as their familiarity of the pattern increases. The Warrior should also practice the Drills with both the left and right hand.

STATIC: SECONDARY POSTURES

Once the standing static training has become comfortable the Warrior should begin to adopt secondary postures from which to train the Cut & Thrust patterns. The Warrior should use their imagination in deciding which posture to use. I personally recommend at a minimum the following postures:

a. On one knee

b. On 2 knees

c. Lying flat on the stomach

d. Lying flat on the back

e. Lying on the right side

f. Lying on the left side

These secondary postures are important to train because unlike the Dojo, in real life a Warrior may find themselves in one of these less favorable positions. The Warrior Should make these postures part of their regular training routine. It is important for the Warrior to become inoculated to these odd postures. The Warrior should make every effort to instinctively function from these postures.

DYNAMIC: ALTERNATING LEADS DRILL

Once the Warrior has become comfortable with the Cut & Thrust patterns in a static setting the Warrior can begin to incorporate movement of the feet and legs. One key drill is the "Alternating Leads" drill. In the Alternating Leads drill the Warrior will choose a Cut & Thrust pattern and adopt a strong side lead. From this lead the Warrior will execute the first movement in their chosen pattern. After the first movement the Warrior will switch leads and execute the second movement in the pattern. The Warrior will continue to alternate their leads for every movement in the pattern. By doing so, the Warrior will begin to assimilate dual the dual motion of the hands and feet. In my opinion this drill alone can be worked at length to great results in the building of skill.

DYNAMIC: WALK ABOUT DRILL

For the Walk About Drill the Warrior should choose any of the Cut & Thrust Patterns and begin to simply walk forwards and backwards while executing the pattern. Foot work should be as natural as possible. Simple foot over foot as if you were walking to the park. The Warrior should follow a training partner who will walk forward, backwards, and on off angles. This drill will allow the Warrior to become comfortable with executing upper body movements while on the move. This drill is a natural progression from Alternating Leads drill.

DYNAMIC: THE SPINNING MAN

For the Spinning Man Drill the Warrior will walk naturally, following their training partner who will slowly spin 360 degrees as they move in order to give the Warrior the opportunity to execute the cutting patterns and overlay them on a body that is in constant motion. The Warrior will have the opportunity to work the cutting patterns on a moving body. This is important because most students will train the patterns while facing a target that is facing them. In combat an enemy may turn, and the Warrior who has not seen this scenario in training may hesitate because they have not experienced this variation in the past.

MAROZZO'S SEGNO

In 1536 Italian fencing Master Achilles Marozzo's book "Opera Nova" was first printed. The manual was one of the most influential fencing manuals of its time and is still studied extensively to this day. In the Opera Nova, Marozzo introduces us to and defines the following Cutting angles. The Warrior can and should practice all of these angles as outlined. Although originally presented as cutting angels, the arrangement works equally well with thrusting techniques. The collection of cutting and thrusting patterns in the Way of the Raven System group these core angles in variety of sequences.

(1) Montante: Vertical upward cut

(2)Ridoppio Rovesa: Ascending diagonal cut from left to right

(3)Tondo Roversa: Horizontal cut from left to right

(4)Squalembratto Roversa: Descending diagonal cut from left to right

(5) Fendente: Vertical Downward Cut

(6) Squalembratto Mandrito: Descending diagonal cut from right to left

(7) Tondo Mandritto: Horizontal cut from right to left

(8) Ridoppio Mandritto: Ascending diagonal cut from right to left

THE MEYER SQUARE

In his Trieste from 1570, The Art of Combat, German Freifechter (free fencer) Joachim Meyer introduces us to the Meyer Square. The Square is a training aid meant to be used primarily with the long sword. The Meyer Square however works equally for the hawk. To begin using the square the Warrior should execute a downward diagonal cut beginning at the "outward" numeral 1. Once the Warrior has cut at the angle of the "outward" 1, they should move on to the angle of the "outward" 2, then 3, then 4. Once the outward numerals have been addressed the Warrior will begin to cut at the second layer, then the third and finally the fourth before beginning the exercise again at the outer layer. This Training aid from the work of free fencer Joachim Meyer gives us a useful tool as well as a glimpse into the training methods of the western blade masters.

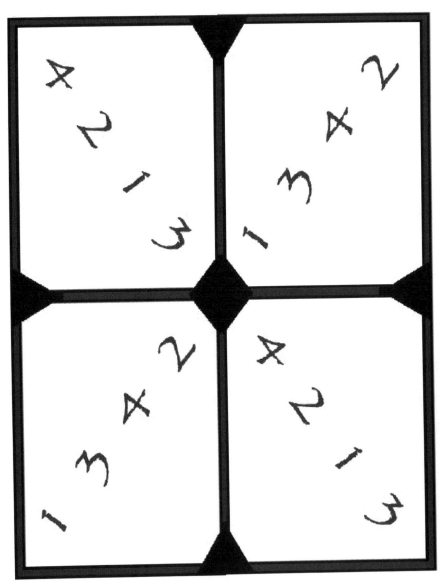

ANATOMY & PHYSIOLOGY

DISABLING TARGETS

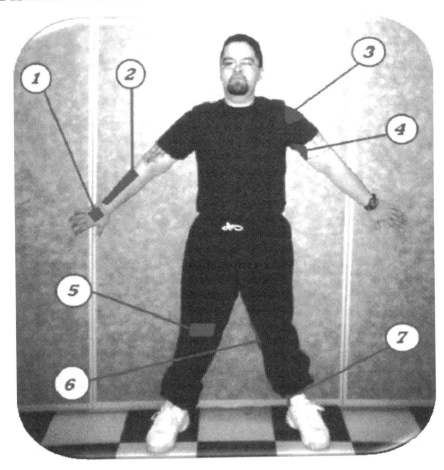

I would now like to take a look at the Coup de Jarnac. Not the Coup de Janich, although it would make sense as he is arguably the foremost expert on biomechanical disabling knife tactics in the field. The Coup de Jarnac is a term that had its birth in France in 1547. A judicial dual in 1547 saw Guy Chabot the Baron de Jarnac face off with François de Vivonne de la Châtaigneraie. Chataigneraie was widely recognized as one of the greatest swordsmen in France. In preparation for the duel Guy Chabot sought out the instruction of Italian fencing Master Captain Caizo. On the day of the dual, Chabot successfully used two disabling cuts to drop the greatest swordsman in France to his knees. Chataigneraie was in effect hamstringed by Chabot. The tactic of disabling rather than killing became widely known as the Coup de Jarnac.

The Coup de Jarnac is an excellent example of a disabling attack. Disabling attacks are those brought to targets that when cut or damaged are most certain to stop or seriously impair mobility or function. Like any wound a disabling attack can be lethal, but is rarely so if medical attention can be acquired in a reasonable amount of time.

Targets will include: *(1) Back of the hand, (2) Back of the forearm, (3) Deltoid, (4) Triceps, (5) Front of the Knee, (6) Back of the knee/hamstring, (7) Achilles tendon*

DELAYED FATALITY

There are targets on the human body which when cut or damaged will result in a more or less certain fatality if not treated immediately. Without proper medical the injured individual will die due to blood loss. The injured party will likely experience light headedness, unconsciousness, and eventually die from blood loss. The rate at which impairment occurs can vary from relatively quick to relatively slow. This means that a Warrior must be aware that even if they have received this type of wound they still have a viable chance of fighting through and controlling the situation. The survival mindset at this point is imperative for the Warrior. Targets will include: *(1) Carotid artery, (2) Sub-clavian artery, (3) Brachial artery, (4) Ulnar artery, (5) Radial artery, (6) Femoral artery, (7) Popliteal artery.*

FAST KILLS

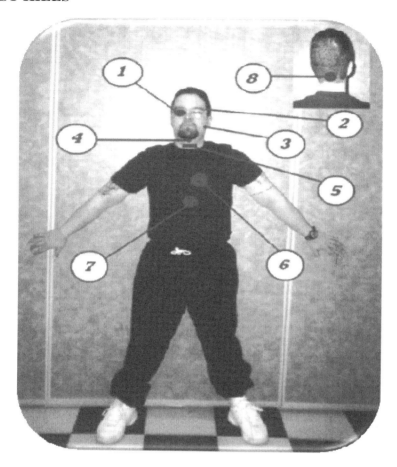

Fast kill targets when cut or damaged will be almost immediately fatal. It is paramount that the Warrior protect these targets areas at all times and at all costs. The sacrificing of another non-vital body part in the protection of these targets is obviously acceptable and should be employed if needed. For example, if a subject stabs at a Warrior's eye, and the Warrior has no option for movement, it would be acceptable for the Warrior to cover their eye sacrificing the hand in order to avoid a fatal wound.

Targets will include: *(1)Brain via eye socket, (2)Brain via temple (3)Brain via space behind the ear (4)Brain via space under the chin (5) throat, (6) heart, (7)Solar Plexus (8) Base of the Skull.*

It is crucial that Warriors learn the edged weapon targets for two reasons:

(1). The Warrior can better protect themselves if they know which parts of their body are the most crucial to protect.

(2). Warriors can better decide appropriately as to what level of force to use since they will have a clear understanding of what their application to each body target will accomplish. Warriors must know what targets are most likely to stop the action of the assault.

CONFLICT PHYSIOLOGY

Research has proven that under conflict stress fine motor skills become impaired. Gross motor skills however are available and in some instances sharpen.

Conflict stress will affect the body in a number of ways. Sensory systems are affected such as vision, and hearing. Motor skill functions will be affected, as well as memory. These effects are can be directly correlated to the person's heart rate. Although there are people who on average have a heart rate much lower or faster at rest than the average person. In general when the heart rate reaches between 115 and 145 beats per minute the body will lose the ability to complete fine or complex motor skills. At about 145 beats per minute, hearing becomes unreliable. A person may have only partial hearing or complete hearing loss altogether. When the body reaches 175 beats per minute it will experience narrow vision or tunnel vision. In this state a person will see in a binocular manner as opposed to the normal monocular state. Visual tracking is also difficult at this stage of heart rate. Memory is also affected once a person reaches this stage. Recall of events which occurred in this stage will be difficult for the person. Above 180 beats per minute the person is likely to enter into a stage of "hyper vigilance". Irrational behavior is common at this stage. Also common is the complete impairment of the individual, often referred to incorrectly as "being in shock" or being frozen. Effects to the system can be managed through proper breathing, and exposure to crisis rehearsal and realistic scenario training drills. Proper breathing is achieved by inhaling on a three second count through the nose holding the breath for 2 seconds and then exhaling the breath on a three second count through the mouth. The person must also utilize conflict rehearsal and visualization to help improve their performance. Realistic drill and scenario training is also a crucial component. Through these two techniques the person can achieve a level of stress inoculation which others will lack.

BREATH CONTROL

"Everyone likes to breath, especially me"
-American Football legend Jim Brown

Breath is life. If you lose control of your breath in combat, well you're likely to lose your life along with it. Let's take a look at two techniques to improve your breathing and improve your odds of coming out on top.

TACTICAL BREATHING

We have discussed the effects that stress can have on one's heart rate. Heart rate can be decreased by using tactical breathing. The lower your heart rate the better chance you have of fighting off the negative effects of stress in combat on your body. Breathe deep, expanding your stomach as you inhale. Each of the following steps should take a four count to complete. The four steps to this breathing are:

- In through the nose, two, three, four.

- Hold two, three, and four.

- Out through the lips two, three, four.

- Hold two, three, four.

This tactical breathing sequence is most effective when repeated at least four times.

BREATHING LIKE A HORSE

One of the most useful things I ever learned in the art of combat was how to breathe like a horse. Horses neigh; they expel a lot of air in one big breath. I learned from Mr. Lopez that this trick helped a lot in sparring. I have faced off with guys with far better conditioning than I have only see them get winded during a long match because they didn't know how to breath. When I would begin to feel that I was losing my wind I would expel one or two big deep puffs. Doing this helped to expel co2 from the body and allowed me to keep moving.

THE PHINEAS GAGE FACTOR

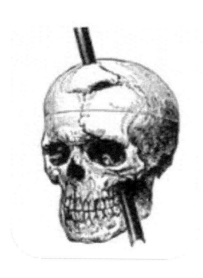

Most of us are famiiar with Murphy's Law. The adage that states that if something can go wrong it normally will. Well, I introduce you all to what I call the Phineas Gage Factor. The Phineas Gage Factor could be thought of as Murphy's Law applied to physical trauma. There are a million "blade experts" in the world that will tell you that if you cut here and wait for 30 seconds the enemy will keel over and die. Knife wound bleed out tables are common, although some are more realistic than others there are still many variables that can effect their predictions, blood pressure, first aid, size, build, etc. A firm knowledge of anatomy can give us a good base of understanding of how the human body may react to trauma. Of all targeting options available to a Warrior, cuts and injuries to the tendons (hamstring, achilles tendon, etc), and deep thrusts to the heart and brain are the most likely to have the desired result. Over the years however through my research I have come to hold the following opinion. We may know what is likely to happen but short of the guillotine, there are no, **ABSOLUTELY NO** Definate out comes.

There are many 99.9% likelihoods but no 100% Absolutes short of a decapitation.

 If you hang aound the blade community or the law enforcement community long enough you will hear stories of bad guys who have suffered incredible amounts of trauma and keep on coming. Most stories are well documented and should be enough to convince you. If you do a google image search for "knife victim" there is a now famous image that will turn up of a man sitting in a hospital gurney. The man had extreme trauma to his back, he looked like a carved thanksgiving turkey. Most people see this and say "see how dangerous a blade can be". I look at it and say " this guy is cut up, but hes awake and alive and sitting upright, the guy that cut him didn't know how to pick his targets, other wise he would be in the morgue not the ER."

In the course of my research I had the opportunity to interview "Punk Rock Annie". Annie was a bartender in one of the cities punk dive bars. Annie was a small thing, standing only 5ft tall and not weighting more than 112lbs. In the course of her career as bar tender Annie had the misfortune of landing herself a stalker. One night after work she got in her car and began to drive. She heard her tires making funny noises. She assumed it was a flat and decided to drive on to the gas station at the corner. Once she got there she got out of the car and realized that all 4 of her tires had been slashed. Annie began speaking to the gas station attendent and all of a sudden she felt what she described as three bumps on her back. Nothing painful, more like little pushes. Just then Annie noticed that her stalker ran past her and acrross the street. She stated that she watched him for what seemed to be a long time before she felt a warm, wet sensation on her backside. Annie said that for a second she felt that she had urinated on herself. It wasn't until she touched her pants and looked that she realized that warm wet sensation was coming from her own blood. Upon seeing her own blood Annie felt faint and collapsed to the ground with a punctured lung and two additional stab wounds. If it had not been for the gas station attendent acting quickly she may not have lived to tell her story. What struck me as interesting is the amount of time that elapsed with no pain until she realized what had happened to her. Annie still contends that she collapsed because the sight of blood scared her not because she was injured.

If all of this does not convince you then to support my opinion I present the case of Phineas P. Gage. Mr. Gage was an American railroad worker in the 1840's. While working an explosion sent a large 13lb iron rod flying through the left side of his face and out the top of his head. The injury it was later discovered had destroyed much of his brain's left <u>frontal lobe</u>. Now most reasonable people would assume that with such an injury Mr. Gage would have died.

Mr. Gage however, convulsed for a moment and then within a few minutes he spoke and with assistance he stood up and walked. Now if there was ever a case to prove that you cannot count 100% on any one injury to terminate your enemy it is this one. A 13lb crowbar through the brain folks. Let me repeat, **"A 13LB CROW BAR THROUGH THE FREAKING BRAIN".** So the next time some blade "expert" tells you that any targeting issue is for certain remind them about the "Phineas Gage Factor".

For additional training in the use of the Tomahawk I recommend the following instructors and their training materials.

Dwight McLemore Macneen@gmail.com	**James Keating** www.Jameskeating.com
Tim Anderson Eskrima66@Hotmail.com	**Pete Kautz** www.AllianceMartialArts.com
David Seiwert www.DynamicFightingArts.com	**Keith Jennings** www.FortezaFitness.com
Fernan Vargas www.FernanVargas.com	**Chad McBroom** www.compfightsys.com
Snake Blocker www.BlockerAcademy.com	**Mark Davies** www.TacticalEdge.co.uk
Raven Cain www.kobura.wix.com/theway	**Lynn Thompson** www.ColdSteel.com
Black Hawk Walters www.kobura.wix.com/theway	**C. Allen Reed** www.GallowGlassAcademy.com

BIBLIOGRAPHY

1. TRADIZIONI SCHERMISTICHE IN LIGURIA E PIEMONTE BY GILBERTO PAUCIULLO & ANTONIO GG MERENDONI

2. INFANTRY SWORD EXERCISE BY HENRY CHARLES ANGELO

3. BROAD SWORD FIGHTING BY PAUL PORTER

4. THE FAIRBAIRN MANUAL OF KNIFE FIGHTING BY WILLIAM L. CASSIDY

5. TREATISE ON FENCING BY MICHAL STARZEWSKI.

6. TEATRO BY NICOLETTO GIGANTI

7. FIGHTING WITH THE SABER BY NORMAN J. FINKELSHTEYN

8. INTRODUCTION TO ITALIAN RAPIER BY DAVID AND DORI COBLENTZ

9. KNIFE HANDELING FOR SELF DEFENSE BY GEORGE B. WALLACE

10. PUT EM DOWN, TAKE EM OUT KNIFE FIGHTING TECHNIQUES FROM FOLSOM PRISON BY DON PENTECOST

11. CLOSE SHAVES THE COMPLETE BOOK OF RAZOR FIGHTING BY BRADLEY J. STEINER

12. A SIMPLIFIED METHOD FOR TEACHING DAGGER TECHNIQUES BY ELI STEENPUT

13. NINJA KNIFE FIGHTING BY R. KELLY HILL JR. M.D.

14. 5 RULES TO EFFECTIVE STREET COMBAT BY ANDREW CURTISS

15. THE SICILIAN BLADE BY VITTO QUATTROCCHI

16. POLICE NON-LETHAL FORCE MANUAL: YOUR CHOICES THIS SIDE OF DEADLY BY BILL CLEDE

17. THE ART AND THE SCIENCE, AN INTRODUCTION TO RAPIER TECHNIQUES OF SALVATOR FABRIS BY PHIL MARSHALL

18. THE DEATH DEALERS MANUAL BY BRADLEY J. STEINER

19. PATH OF THE RONIN BY KEVIN SECOURS

20. RENAISSANCE RAPIER TECHNIQUE AND TACTICS BY JOSEPH "BLAYDE" BRICKY

21. OLD SWORD PLAY BY ALFRED HUTTON

22. PRISON KILLING TECHNIQUES BY RALF DEAN OMAR

23. HONOR, MASCULINITY, AND RITUAL KNIFE FIGHTING IN NINETEENTH-CENTURY GREECE BY THOMAS GALLANT

24. GREAT REPRESENTATION OF THE ART AND USE OF FENCING BY RIDOLFO CAPO FERRO OF CAGLI

25. PERSPECTIVES ON MALICIA BY SHAYNA MCHUGH

26. FENCING BY WALTER H. POLLOCK, F.C. GROVE & CAMILLE PREVOST.

27. RARE DAGGER TECHNIQUES FROM AN ANONYMOUS MANUAL BY PETE KAUTZ

28. THE GUINNESS BOOK OF MILITARY ANECDOTES BY GEOFFREY REAGAN

29. THE SPANISH CIRCLE GIRARD THIBAULT'S CIRCLE DIAGRAM AN EXAMINATION OF THE MYSTERIES, BACKGROUND AND PERIOD USE OF THE SPANISH CIRCLE ALSO KNOWN AS LA DESTREZAS RESEARCHED BY HL JOHN JAMES MACCRIMMON

30. THE ONE KNIFE FIGHT OF JIM BOWIE PARADOXES OF A MYTH BY LT COL. DWIGHT MCLEMORE

31. BACK CUT-THE BURTON MYSTIQUE BY JOHN BEDNARSKI

32. EVOLUTION OF THE USMC BIDDLE METHOD BY DANIEL TREMBULA

33. MEYER DAGGER PLAYS VERSION BY JASON VAIL

34. MILITARY GEOLOGY AND THE APACHE WARS, SOUTH WEST UNITED STATES BY PETER DOYLE

35. MANUAL DI COMPLEMENT AL COMBATTIMENTO INDIVIDUALE PER GLI ESERCITI BY ANTONIO G.G. MERENDONI

36. THE APACHES: AMERICA'S GREATEST GUERILLA FIGHTERS BY BLAISE LOONG

37. MCRP 3-02B CLOSE COMBAT U.S. MARINE CORPS

38. FM 21-150 COMBATIVES US ARMY

39. PREMIERE MARTIAL ARTS OF UNIVERSAL CITY TEXAS LEADERSHIP MANUAL TOM & JUANITA HOWANIC

40. SLASH & THRUST BY JOHN SANCHEZ

41. BLADE MASTER BY JOHN SANCHEZ

42. MONADNOCK DEFENSIVE TACTICS SYSTEM MANUAL JOSEPH TRUNCALE & TERRY E. SMITH

43. STUDENT FENCING GUIDE BY ALFRED LOUIE

44. COLD STEEL BY ALFRED HUTTON

45. ESSENTIALS OF FENCING TECHNIQUE BY RICHARD HOWARD

46. HAND WORK FOR DUELING BY LARRY TOM

47. INTRODUCTION TO THE MEDIEVAL LONG SWORD BY THE CHICAGO SWORD PLAY GUILD

48. DAGA, BY CHRISTOPHER PENNEY & NICHOLAS CONWAY

49. THE ANNOTATED FABRIS BY KRISTOPHE SPRENGER

50. TRATTO DI SCIENZIA D'ARMES, BY CAMILLO AGRIPPA

51. OPERA NOVA BY ACHILLES MAROZZO'S

52. THE ART OF COMBAT BY JOACHIM MEYER

53. THE BOOK OF MORMON BY JOSEPH SMITH

54. GREAT REPRESENTATION OF THE ART AND USE OF FENCING BY RIDOLFO CAPO FERRO

55. UNDERSTANDING TEMPO BY TOMMASO LEONI

56. SEVILLIAN STEEL BY JAMES LORIEGA

57. PARADOXES OF DEFENCE BY GEORGE SILVER

58. BRIEF INSTRUCTIONS ON MY PARADOXES OF DEFENCE BY GEORGE SILVER

59. COLD STEEL BY ALFRED HUTTON

60. FROM THE PAGE TO THE PRACTICE, FUNDAMENTALS OF SPANISH SWORDPLAY BY PUCK CURTIS AND MARY DILL CURTIS.

61. THE BOOK OF MARTIAL POWER BY PROFESSOR STEVEN J. PEARLMAN

62. 20 ESSENTIALS YOU NEED TO KNOW ABOUT USING AND DEFENDING AGAINST COLD STEEL BY LYNN THOMPSON

63. SLEIGHT OF HAND IN KNIFE FIGHTING BY JAMES SASS

64. MASTERING YANG STYLE TAIJIAUAN BY ZHONGWEN FU

65. THE TRUE MEANING OF JU IN JUDO AND JUJITSU BY ANDREW VIANNAKIS PHD AND LINDA VIANNAKIS M.S.

66. FOX WALKING AND WIDE ANGLE VISION BY PAUL SCHEITER

67. BOOK OF FIVE RINGS BY MUSASHI

68. APACHE KNIFE FIGHTING & BATTLE TACTICS VOLUME II BY SNAKE BLOCKER

69. APACHE KNIFE FIGHTING & BATTLE TACTICS VOLUME III BY SNAKE BLOCKER

70. APACHE KNIFE FIGHTING & BATTLE TACTICS VOLUME I BY SNAKE BLOCKER

71. THE SCHOOL OF FENCING BY MR. ANGELO

72. ARCHERY, FENCING, AND BROADSWORD BY "STONEHENGE," AND THE REV. J. G. WOOD.

73. FM-23-25 WAR DEPARTMENT BASIC FIELD MANUAL: BAYONET

74. NINJA COMBAT METHOD BY STEPHEN HAYES

75. KNIFE FIGHTING, KNIFE THROWING FOR COMBAT BY MICHAEL ECHANIS

76. PRISON'S BLOODY IRON BY HAROLD J. JENKS AND MICHAEL H. BROWN

77. MILITARY KNIFE FIGHTING BY ROBERT K. SPEAR

78. RAPIER FUNDAMENTALS BY DARREN DI BATTISTA

79. EPEE TEMPO BY COACH ALLEN EVANS

80. THE SECOND INTENTION TACTIC IN GERMAN FECHBUCH OF 16TH CENTURY BY GEORGE E. GEORGAS

ABOUT THE AUTHOR
FERNAN VARGAS

 Mr. Vargas is a lifelong martial artist who currently holds a *Menkyo Kaiden* in Bushi Satori Ryu as well as black belts and instructor rankings in Kuntao, Silat, Kuntaw, Jujutsu and Hapkido. As a certified Law Enforcement Defensive Tactics Instructor, Mr. Vargas has taught defensive tactics to law enforcement officers at the local, state, and federal level, as well as security officers, military personnel and private citizens from around the United States and foreign nations such as Canada, Italy, and Spain. Mr. Vargas has developed programs which have been approved by the Police officer training and Standards Board of several states, and adopted by agencies such as the Pentagon Force protection Agency. Additionally, organizations such as the Fraternal Order of Law Enforcement and the International Academy of Executive Protection Agents have given formal endorsements of the programs developed by Mr. Vargas and Raven Tactical International. Mr. Vargas has been an instructor at the prestigious International Law Enforcement Educators & Trainers Association International Conference (ILEETA). Mr. Vargas currently holds instructor credentials in over 20 defensive tactics and combatives curriculums.

As an author Mr. Vargas has published several books on topics such as *Law Enforcement Defensive Tactics*, *Knife Combatives*, the *Tomahawk*, *Native American Fighting Traditions*, *Crime Survival*, and more. His writings have also appeared in numerous Industry periodicals.

Fernan Vargas is a current Safety Patrol Leader and Trainer for the Chicago Chapter of the Guardian Angels Safety Patrol where he has worked on several high profile anti-crime campaigns. Mr. Vargas is the founder of the official *Guardian Angels Defensive Tactics System*. A program used to teach Guardian Angels and the public alike. Mr. Vargas and the Guardian Angels have demonstrated the *Guardian Angels Defensive Tactics System* for various television stations including WGN Chicago, Telemundo, ABC Chicago, WCIU Chicago, and NBC Chicago

Mr. Vargas has dedicated a significant portion of his career to the study of edged weapons. He is recognized as an edged weapon subject matter expert; Mr. Vargas holds instructor rankings in several edged weapons curriculums ranging from Native American knife combatives, Kali, Military knife combatives, and several others. He is the only American to be granted the title of *Soma de Cutel* by Grand Master Gilberto Pauciullo and the Instituto per le Tradisioni Marziali Italiane. Mr. Vargas has also been awarded the honorific title of *Master Knife Instructor* by his Sifu David Siewert and the designation of *Mater at Arms* by Ernest Emerson and the Order of the Black Shamrock.

Mr. Vargas was named *Trainer of the Year* 2011 by the Alliance of Guardian Angels and has been inducted in several halls of fame for his instruction of Defensive Tactics and Combatives. Mr. Vargas has been inducted into several Martial Arts Halls of Fame and has been awarded the Presidential Service Award and the Shinja Buke Ryu Humanitarian Award for service to the community.

www.TheRavenTribe.com

www.RavenTactical.com

www.RavenTalkPodcast.com

www.MartialBooks.com

www.FernanVargas.com

Made in the USA
Middletown, DE
11 July 2021